Foreword by Canon John Hugh

This is the story of a wife and mother wh(
Ghana to this country and discovered her marriage was breaking up, leaving her with four children to look after, no home, no secure income to purchase a home or a job to provide for her family.

It is a remarkable story of a journey through pain which brought about personal growth and eventually a ministry to international students and their wives that was to be very significant.

Jill has made such a journey through sorrow and tears but has discovered the grace of God to forgive, to find healing, to find provision for her family and to welcome others into her home.

It is a wonderful story of hospitality that reveals the hospitality of God. The German word for hospitality is 'gastfreundschaft' which means friendship for a guest. Hospitality, therefore, means primarily the creation of a free space where the stranger can enter and become a friend instead of a stranger. Hospitality is not to change people, but to offer them a space where change can take place. It is opening up an opportunity for others to find God in their own way.

This is what I see in Jill's story that will be such an encouragement to others that God can work all things together for good, if we but listen to his promptings and follow them.

Canon John Hughes
February 2011

John Hughes was Vicar of St John's Harborne, Birmingham, from 1992 to 2009.

LAVENDER IN THE DRAWERS

Jill Edgington

Morse-Brown
Publishing

First published in the United Kingdom in 2011
by Morse-Brown Publishing
506F The Big Peg, 120 Vyse Street, Birmingham B18 6NE

All rights reserved

© 2011 by Jill Edgington

This book is sold subject to the condition that it shall not, by way of trade or otherwise, be lent, resold, hired out or otherwise circulated without the publisher's prior consent in any form of binding or cover other than that in which it is published and without a similar condition including this condition being imposed on the subsequent purchaser.

ISBN: 978-1-907615-04-7

Scripture quotations taken from the Holy Bible, New International Version.
Copyright © 1973, 1978, 1984 by the International Bible Society.
Used by permission of Hodder & Stoughton,
a member of the Hodder Headline Group.
All rights reserved.

Contents

1. Why?
2. Curriculum Vitae
3. Utter Worthlessness
4. When God Steps in to Heal
5. Four Kids and a Pound
6. Back into Teaching
7. Disbelief
8. The Beginning of Miracles
9. Money Matters
10. Lavender in the Drawers
11. 'I Need You to be More Available'
12. Getting Going
13. Using One's Home
14. It's Tuesday – Do Come and Join Us
15. Setting a Pattern
16. Seeing Individual Lives Blessed
17. Hindrances along the Way
18. Upheaval
19. God Who Blesses

ONE

Why?

I settled down in my seat on the suburban train waiting at Waterloo Station, a toddler squirming on my lap. As the train was about to leave the platform a smartly dressed middle-aged businessman stepped up into the carriage, stumbled past me, brushing my knees, and then sat down opposite. The train pulled out of the station as he leant across to ask if he was on the right train for Bromley. As I told him that he would have to change at the next station, he suddenly blurted out that he was blind! In the next three minutes I listened to the bare facts of his sudden blindness nine months previously and the ensuing bitterness, ending with a cry from the heart: 'Why the hell should God let this happen to me?'

And I, a Christian since my teenage years, so well-taught in biblical doctrine, had nothing to say! I remained silent as the train came to a halt, because that was my bitter question, and I had no answer to give that man as I helped him off the train and onto the platform. I continued my journey home to south-east London knowing that that stranger had verbalised the question hidden in my heart that desperately needed an answer and I could no longer keep it a secret and pretend it wasn't there. That brief encounter started to turn my life around. I had to face my own problems rather than pretend they did not exist.

This book is not an account of those problems, nor of the many painful years that led up to them. Nor is it the story of one who survived; but it is an offering of praise to the one who led me through and has given me so much more than I ever dreamed possible. And it is written for others going through long, dark tunnels for whatever reason. If you need to be encouraged and reassured that there is a God who cares and to whom each one of us is infinitely precious, then I offer glimpses of encouragement for those who specially need it – just now. Thirty-nine years later he still whispers to me: '*You are precious and honoured… and I love you!*'

And he says the same to you! I offer the reality of a Saviour and Lord to those who desperately need the peace and joy and love, often in unexpected places or through unknown people, that he has given me.

TWO

Curriculum Vitae

As the Second World War was ending, I was sent by my parents to a girls' public boarding school in Gloucestershire for six years, where I made friends, enjoyed various sports and took the usual examinations. It was while at school that I decided to read the Bible through to see if there was more to the Christian faith than just 'church-going' and singing hymns. I was hungry for so much more. It was on 8 February 1948 that, as I was reading Revelation chapter 3 verse 20, my life was transformed: 'Behold, I stand at the door, and knock: if anyone hears my voice and opens the door, I will come in to him, and will sup with him and he with me.' I realised that there was a personal relationship to be enjoyed and I entered that relationship there and then in my boarding school dormitory. Life was never to be the same again! I knew Christ in a personal way that changed everything.

I gained a place at university to read History and then had what today would be considered a 'gap year' until I was old enough to take my university place. I tasted something of the world of work and also travelled with my parents to the Eastern Mediterranean. Did this begin to interest me in cross-cultural relationships? While at London University I met my future husband, for we were both on the committee of the college branch of the London Inter-Faculty Christian Union. I think we 'fell in love' at university and, when we had both finished our courses, we married, living in rented accommodation in Kent. I stepped inside a state school for the first time in my life when I started to teach in a grammar school in Kent.

It seemed after a while that God was calling us to work overseas, so we offered to work in newly independent Ghana, which was asking for professional help there at that time. I found myself helping to set up an international school in Kumasi where we were living, and teaching a very multi-national class for some time. After four years we returned to Britain for a year to adopt our first child and then we moved on to Tanzania which had recently gained its independence. By this time we had two adopted small children, but in the evenings I helped to teach English to adults. We lived in northern Tanzania, close to Mount Kilimanjaro, but also travelled considerably in other African countries and learned much about cross-cultural differences. It was while living in Tanzania that 'cracks' started to appear in our marriage. I was floundering in an area where I didn't know how to cope, with another person forming an adulterous relationship with my husband.

After another four years, we returned to Britain and I believed that 'forgive and forget' was the best way forward. We settled in Eltham, where my husband had a job as a lecturer in a teacher-training college. After adopting a third child, I suddenly found that I was pregnant after all those years. I was hoping that all might be well in our marriage, when I discovered to my horror that my husband had formed a relationship with a research worker at the college. I survived this 'tangle' for some time until finally 'going public', finding myself unable to cope with this new threesome, and eventually headed for Birmingham with four small children – and a tank full of petrol!

The rest is referred to in this book. I am still in Birmingham, having taught here for a number of years. Then came a dramatic call to leave teaching and work 'full-time' with international families, of whom there are so many near where I live, and many of whom are so lonely. So here I am with an open home and many, many contacts! God uses the most unlikely people to reach out to others! I am one of those unlikely ones!

It is hoped that this book would reach Christians who are really struggling with hard times for whatever reason and who need encouragement that the Lord will see them through whatever they are facing, and actually bless them in the process. I meet so many who are finding their particular circumstances so difficult and who long for encouragement along their way. May this touch a few aching hearts with a sense of reassurance and blessing.

He heals the broken-hearted and binds up their wounds. (Psalm 147: 3)

THREE

Utter Worthlessness

As I tried yet again to win a husband back from long years of unfaithfulness, I knew that I was totally unworthy. If I had been different, if I had been more attractive, then this would never have happened, and I would not yet again have the heavy burden of hopelessness weighing down on my shoulders. But I was a 'failure' who was unable to maintain a sound, positive relationship with my husband of a number of years. Instead I was to blame for the drifting apart that had now become obvious to the two of us, even if it was hidden from the outside world. The spontaneous joy and sense of fun had slowly ebbed away leaving a void that other people filled, and I was the one to blame! And I felt the shame of this very deeply, but I didn't know how to put it right.

I was busy running a home and looking after young children and I didn't know how to retrieve the sparkle that I had lost in the process. I was dreary and unattractive and not often available to go out for the evening because baby-sitters were expensive and hard to come by, and so I allowed the inevitable gap to widen even more. I was often tired and I didn't know how to regain the energy that I had lost. I was more desperate than friends around us ever realised. Life seemed to be so pointless and I could not see a way out, for there just wasn't one. Some friends who could see what was happening warned me about the trap I was in, but I couldn't see a way to escape.

Yet there we were, a respectable couple in our local church, without people realising what was happening underneath, until I burst the bubble by acting on the advice of a friend and going to my local pastor and sharing something of what was really happening, with my husband the worship leader in the church, and I leading the work amongst the many young people. And that pastor was brilliant in his counselling and care and did all he could to help to repair the broken relationship. Yes, at the time we were blessed with a church leader who was greatly gifted with wise advice and persistence in his care. We were so blessed in this, but in the end I was shocked when he told me much later that he believed that eventually I would have to go – and it proved true a year later, and I found myself on the move and uprooted.

But first I tried everything I knew to redeem the situation. I took a part-time job back in my old career of teaching so that I could not be accused of just spending and not contributing to the family budget. I tried to listen to the advice of those around about giving the extra to a relationship that desperately needed the healing that I could not find. I acted as chauffeur when my husband lost his driving licence. I sought to forgive – though I could never accept as right – the 'threesome' that I found myself tangled up in. How many others have found it impossible to accept another person pushing in – even into the home – in a way that undermines that special relationship between husband and wife? I even had six weeks of a younger, much more attractive woman living under our roof – and that seemed impossibly hard. For I knew perfectly well who the favoured one was. And I was the 'has been' who didn't seem to stand a chance. When others find themselves in this position, never accept the lies that this would not have happened if only you had been a better wife, for that way leads inevitably to self-condemnation and desperate hopelessness. I knew the agony of a breaking heart while at the same time seeking to repair and find God's healing for a relationship and also give the children a sense of normality. In future years I was to understand all too well those I came across battling to restore a shattered relationship; for I had been there before and I knew the agony of watching the disintegration of a relationship that had meant so much in the past.

FOUR

When God Steps in to Heal

Bitterness, especially when it has gone very deep, is one of the most devastating of human emotions. It seems to lie dormant, sometimes for long periods of time, and then someone or some situation once more triggers what is really underneath, and the hurt and the pain come out with a deadly venom, apparently for no real reason, and those nearby are shocked at the passionate outburst. It is an emotion that seems to drive the one infected into a desolate wilderness where the chill winds of self-pity whip round one in an icy grip and, although on the surface most of the time life seems to be going along at its usual pace, underneath there is a deadly misery that no one else can ever possibly understand.

Why has life treated me like this? Why me of all people? What has happened to all the joy that used to be there? How could anyone else understand? Others seem to be so carefree and life hasn't dealt them such a cruel blow. And, anyway, where's God in all this? He is never very real when one is drifting in a misty, pathless wilderness. He is far away and he doesn't care. I am living a life of pretence and I am too tired and too preoccupied with my personal survival to try to find a way out. There's a daily routine to be endured; there are ordinary, laughing people to brush shoulders with, and hope I've put on a good enough face so that they will never guess how I'm really feeling. I'm hurting, Lord! And each time there is another rough encounter, the knife seems to twist in the wound and make the pain even more unbearable, and it's no good turning to anyone else, because no one would ever understand the sheer agony of my bitter heart . . . and underneath I've long since given up on God being real in all this!

What triggers the beginning of the healing process? I don't know. I wasn't consciously looking for the healing of my own personal bitterness, when God stepped in one evening. The house was quiet that Saturday evening; four children slept soundly upstairs; I needed to prepare for visitors the next day. As I took a freshly baked cake out of the oven and carefully put it on the worktop to cool, God was suddenly there in my kitchen. I knew, without a shadow of doubt, that God had come to meet with me; there was a glory that I had never known in that way before that shone in that kitchen and I could only bow in worship over the worktop and acknowledge that the Lord himself had come to meet me in the place that was usually full of bustle and activity, but at this moment was strangely still as his presence filled the whole room. And when the sense of glory had finally faded, I realised that he had brought his warmth and joy to my cold, aching inner-being, and I was healed! That terrible bitterness had gone, and all the questions were now irrelevant, because God had come to touch and to breathe his Holy Spirit into every part of my being, and his peace was tangible and all around me – and I stayed where I was, bowed over the kitchen worktop, just accepting that God was so near and he had come to put my life back together again and set my feet back on a Rock, so that I would no longer wander in my bleak, self-imposed, desolate wilderness.

I don't know how long I stayed there, but the sense of awe and reverence was overwhelming and timeless, and I just welcomed the long-forgotten warmth of his presence that seemed to reach to every part of my being. And when I finally left that room, I was walking hand-in-hand with my God, and I knew I was his child again, washed and cleansed from the bitterness and healed.

And so, when I finally stepped out of the kitchen and he gently laid the burden on me to pray for the one who had caused so much of the misery and ensuing bitterness, then I knew it was his burden and that I must take it up in prayer for as long as it would take. And I took that burden gladly, hardly knowing what it would involve in the years ahead. Yes, there is the reality of a 'prayer-burden' that needs to be accepted until it is finally answered. I was given a vivid picture of a husband bowed down and on his knees in repentance that I am still waiting to see fulfilled many years later. I still wait to hear of a repentance that is real and life-changing and the prayer of all these years will have been answered at last. It will happen one day, and I shall be the first to rejoice and to know that this particular burden has been lifted.

Six weeks later I was ready at last and able to step out with a new sense of God's presence in my life to see what God was going to do now. Little did I know how he was going to take the years of hurt and hopelessness and use them in ways I could never have guessed! God never wastes anything he has allowed us to go through, as I say to many different people again and again in these days.

FIVE

Four Kids and a Pound

As I headed north with four children in the car – and a tank full of petrol – little did I know what on earth I was going to do. I had phoned old friends from East African days to ask if I could come. 'Good! Are you coming for a few days' holiday?' they asked. 'Not exactly,' I replied. 'I'm coming because I need to get away. My marriage has broken.'

'Well, come anyway!' they said. Typical African hospitality carried over into my landing in Birmingham! They had tried long before to help me sort out the mess to no avail, and so they were not entirely surprised when I arrived on their doorstep with four young, uprooted children. I had exactly £1 in my purse, but lack of money was the last of my worries just then. I was in a state of shock, and so were my children, and Birmingham was completely unknown territory. I came originally from the south and my children had been removed from a very pleasant, well-mannered primary school in south-east London, to be put into a very different school at the end of that half-term week. They found their new educational environment not what they had experienced before. What on earth was I inflicting on my children? I was incapable of thinking more than a step at a time. My world had fallen apart, and I had no idea what would happen next.

I managed to draw a little money from our bank account until that source of revenue was closed. I phoned a retired couple in Tewkesbury. He had been my pastor when I was a teenager and had later married us when we had both finished at university. Now in retirement they had a godly wisdom that I knew I needed to seek. I was desperate, so I was shocked when they said in reply to my urgent phone-call: 'Come down and see us next Tuesday.' I had thought that I would be offered immediate advice, but here I was told to wait four days!

When I finally went to see them I was so blessed, for they knew exactly what had happened, and in my raw, lacerated state I didn't have to explain anything; they just knew and were able to minister to me in a deep, personal way. When, at a much later time, I asked them how they had known so much of what had happened they explained quite simply that they had spent the intervening days since my phone call just waiting on God for his wisdom in this situation. It taught me much, much later to allow God time to speak, particularly about a difficult matter, and not to rush in with shallow, man-centred advice. The giving of truly godly wisdom is rare, but very precious. Allowing God time to speak into a situation and to act as only he can is so very much needed today.

Yes, in the months to come I knew I could rely on this elderly couple, living in retirement from Christian ministry, to offer such wise counsel. They taught me so much about godly discernment that is all too rare these days. How I praise God for such a gift of calm, loving, older friends like that! We can so easily rush in and out of each other's lives, with one eye on the clock, and offer quick, easy answers, when someone desperately needs that sense that the Lord is there to help and to heal, and that may well take a much longer time. This dear couple taught me so much in those early days about taking time to wait on God.

Time and again I would drive down to Tewkesbury to seek gentle, godly wisdom that helped me to stay on the right path when all around confusing, conflicting voices were offering a welter of advice. It was they who said some time later: 'You need to find your own home, so that you are free to shut your own front door and put your feet up on the mantelpiece if you want to!'

SIX

Back into Teaching

'I hear you are in Birmingham; do you want a job?' So said a headmistress I had never met before over the phone one day early in my time in Birmingham.

'I don't know, and I am in no state for an interview,' I replied in that early, shell-shocked day.

'Well, just come and see if you like the look of us,' replied this amazing head-teacher.

I went over to East Birmingham to a school the like of which I had never closely encountered before. I felt as though I was stepping back in time to Dickens' day, but the warmth of welcome shone through as this incredible headmistress showed me proudly round her girls' secondary school overlooking the Blues football ground. I had come from a completely different background, and here was this woman saying: 'I sum up people quickly and I want you on my staff!' There were incredibly protracted negotiations with the education authority, for they were not prepared to employ any more part-time teachers at that time because the ratio of part-timers was already too high. I knew I could not possibly work full-time with four children to settle into school. That headmistress phoned the education authority every day saying she wanted me on her staff. Eventually I found myself working part-time – hours to suit myself – for the best headmistress I had ever worked for. She was a firm disciplinarian whose care for both staff and pupils shone through. She showed a warmth and encouragement that I needed so desperately as I gradually eased my way back into a teaching community. How gracious of my God to put me into a school like that – one of the first state secondary schools to be built in Birmingham in the nineteenth century: outside toilets, the department where I worked across two playgrounds from the main building, girls who were often from incredibly difficult circumstances, but a warmth of encouragement, notably from my own head of department, that helped me to become re-established in my profession. When I would say 'I can't do that', she would reply: 'Yes, you can!'

She was a 'gem', and my God knew that she was exactly right to lead me back into teaching in those early, insecure days. What an amazing God we have, who cares about the smallest detail, like where I should teach! My head of department kept her poodle under her desk while she taught, and some of the girls exercised her dog for her in the lunch-hour. She had the thoughtfulness to invite me and four hectic children for walks with her – and dog! – on the Lickey or Clent Hills at weekends. She declared herself an agnostic and I was a committed Christian, and God used that woman to give me some adult companionship when I needed just that. I found that God could easily bring non-Christians across my path to give me the support and encouragement that I cried out for, and I in my narrowness beforehand had believed that only committed Christians could be used in that way! We had some wonderful afternoon romps in all weathers, with no difficult questions asked, and just genuine friendship offered.

SEVEN

Disbelief

I came back one evening to the couple where I and the children were staying in Birmingham to find both of them waiting for me in their kitchen. They had something very important to talk over with me, and I was certainly not ready at all for what they were going to say. I had no forewarning of the 'bombshell' that was about to be dropped on me who was struggling to sort out my future in due course.

'We have been talking together about your situation and feel that you will never manage to bring up four children on your own. You have not got what it takes and you are just not the right sort of person. We therefore suggest that we would take the two oldest children off you and we would bring them up and send them to a Christian boarding school. You would then only have to bring up the two younger children, which would be more possible for you. We would, however, make it clear that you should agree never to see the older children again. They would be our responsibility entirely.' I knew instinctively that this was not the right way forward. For better or worse my children belonged together and I loved them all. My oldest son had already been physically chastised by the husband for apparent 'rudeness' and had attempted to run away, and I had had to go and find him and bring him back – fortunately he had not got very far, and anyway he had no idea where to go.

Now I was devastated, for any belief that eventually we could settle down to a relatively normal home-life was totally undermined. I went upstairs to bed utterly broken-hearted. Was there nothing in life that I could manage to do? Yet again, I was a total failure, and I knew I was at rock-bottom. It was the only time that I wept right through the night. My heart was literally breaking; my mind could not comprehend that friends who had taken me in at my time of need were now making a suggestion that would prove yet again how utterly useless I was! I shook with deep weeping. There was no sleep to be had – just a brokenness that made me ache in body, mind and spirit. And in the morning, as I reached for my Bible that I could hardly read with such blood-shot eyes, the Lord himself met me. I turned to Isaiah chapter 54 and God spoke to me afresh just there. It was so personal, and it was for me. There was promise after promise there, each exactly fitting my situation and giving me the fresh hope that I so desperately needed:

> '*Do not be afraid; you will not suffer shame.*
> *Do not fear disgrace; you will not be humiliated.*
> *You will forget the shame of your youth*
> *And remember no more the reproach of your widowhood.*' *(verse 4)*
> '*The Lord will call you back*
> *as if you were a wife deserted and distressed in spirit –*
> *a wife who married young,*
> *only to be rejected,' says your God.*' *(verse 6)*
> '*Though the mountains be shaken*
> *and the hills be removed,*
> *yet my unfailing love for you will not be shaken*
> *nor my covenant of peace be removed,*'
> *says the Lord who has compassion on you.*' *(verse 10)*
> '*O afflicted city, lashed by storms and not comforted,*
> *I will build you with stones of turquoise,*
> *your foundations with sapphires.*
> *I will make your battlements of rubies,*
> *your gates of sparkling jewels,*
> *and all your walls of precious stones.*
> *All your sons will be taught by the Lord,*
> *and great will be your children's peace.*' (verses 11–13)

What an amazing God we have, who speaks to us so clearly through his Word, as though my situation was known when Isaiah originally was called to write those words so long beforehand. Those who are going through deep, deep waters of affliction, as I was then, turn to God's Word and find him speaking so personally just to you there. Turn back to that passage that God has given you time and again when you are tempted to forget what he has already shown you and remember that it is especially for you in your time of need. He is an incredibly personal God when he uses his Word so clearly just like that. Isaiah chapter 54 is my chapter, and I don't know how many, many times I have turned back to that passage in time of need.

Find your special passage in God's Word – ask God to show you – and hold on to his promises there no matter what – for he will bring you through. We have a God who goes with us through the deepest storms, even when we feel he is not there, and who brings us out the other side knowing him more intimately than ever before. He is a God who cares for each one of his children in a way that is completely unique just for you! At 'rock-bottom' our feet touch solid Rock and we are held secure by one who knows exactly what we are going through and who will still lead us out.

EIGHT

The Beginning of Miracles

When I sought the advice of my friends at Tewkesbury they said immediately: 'You must find your own home where you can bring all your children up yourself.' So I started to look, and to ask God to provide, for I needed more than the £1 I had so often in my purse. I needed some financial security, which I did not have, and I needed God's guidance.

Buying a house – if I could – would mean no turning back from living in Birmingham and the break would be much more permanent. At this point I asked God for a very specific sign: if it was right to buy a house, which was impossible financially anyway, I asked that God would seal the buying of the house on my next birthday in January. I believe there are some important occasions when we can be very specific in our request to God. I still possess the letter dated the day before my birthday stating that I could now go ahead and sign for the completion of the purchase. That letter arrived on my birthday. God was so specific in his answer.

The finances were another matter! I now had a part-time teaching post which offered some security, but I calculated that I needed about £2,500 to cover the down-payment, legal fees and basic furnishing. I simply had not any of that, but I had found a house that seemed so suitable and felt 'right' when I walked in, when some friends far away offered to lend me a lump sum of money! 'How much do you want?' they asked. I made a rough calculation and suggested £2,500. 'Just let us know when you want it. You can pay it back when you can. We are not in a hurry.' What an amazing God we have to provide such generous friends like this at such a time!

A house had come on the market because the previous owners had both died within a fortnight of each other. It was incredibly full of their left-behind clutter and it needed some basic modernising. As I stood in the front-room – and there was only one small space to stand because everywhere else was full of old furniture and piles of newspapers – I knew instinctively that this was the right house for me and my children. The house was very close to the University; the significance of its location I didn't realise until many years later. When we look back and recall such times so vividly we often see how it was only God who saw what the future would hold. We have no idea at the time!

NINE

Money Matters

So, with a loan from friends, I had just enough to put down the bare minimum on a house, and gained a mortgage from a very trusting building society. I gleaned a little money from the previous home that was eventually sold in the south, but nowhere near enough to begin to repay the loan. I learned quite quickly that trying to squeeze money out of an unwilling partner does more harm than good to personal relationships. It is almost better to let the whole matter go and see what God plans instead. That is much more difficult and scary in some ways, but dragging finance through the courts seems to leave a residue of bitterness. Within eight months enough gifts, small and large, had come to me to repay my friends' original loan. The last amount sent was an anonymous gift of £500, and to this day I still have no idea who sent it! When people are touched by an amazing God they can be incredibly generous. I certainly found that to be so again and again.

Bringing up four children on somewhat inadequate resources taught me time and again that we have a God who is always faithful, but not necessarily in the way we exactly expect. Yes, I guess I had enough for the basics most of the time, but not always. There was one day I remember well when I came home from teaching just before the children arrived back from school. I knew that I had nothing in the house to make an evening meal for all of us and had no money to go out and buy what we would need. As the children came in from school I felt we were really at the end of our resources. I was just wondering what to do when an envelope came through the front door with £50 inside. I have no idea who the anonymous donor was, but it was more than sufficient to send my oldest child hastily to the local shops to buy what we needed for that evening, and to have some over for the next day. It taught me to pray a blessing on the unknown donor and to thank the Lord who yet again knew our every need. Whether we were relatively affluent or scraping along the bottom, I hope I was beginning to learn to hold whatever I had at the time responsibly, for I had children to provide for, but also to hold my resources open-handed before my God for him to use as he saw fit – and that was sometimes hard, when I felt I had very little compared with others around. I have often needed to remind myself that my Father has 'the cattle on a thousand hills' and he therefore has abundant resources from which to provide for us. But that is sometimes difficult to remember when there is nothing in the larder!

TEN

Lavender in the Drawers

'I've just finished decorating for a couple who are changing their bedroom furniture and would offer their old bedroom furniture to you for free. Would you like it?' So said the man now doing a little decorating for me.

'Oh yes, please,' I replied; for anything useful was not to be turned down. These were early days of trying to bring a home together and furnish it. So I gladly received two wardrobes and a dressing-table that had already seen many years of service. But they were solid and would see many more years of usefulness. I put the smaller wardrobe and the dressing-table in my own small bedroom and opened the top long dressing-table drawer to put away some of my clothes. That drawer was beautifully lined with clean lining paper and on top of the paper was lovingly laid sprigs of lavender. Yes, this was that extra touch from God that reinforced to me that God gives more than we ever expect. I might have had just a cleaned-out drawer, but those simple sprigs of lavender to scent the clothes meant so much more. I stood there just accepting that my God gives over and above what we could ever imagine. Those sprigs of lavender just spoke to me of the extra touches that God so often gives his children to emphasise in such a clear way that he is a God who delights to give his children so much more than we could ever expect. To me it was like that extra-special sunset when the whole horizon is lit up with that brilliant deep red, or the very precious first bloom of a spring flower after a long, drab winter.

As I stood there in my bedroom in front of the opened drawer, I met again with such an amazing God, and it was a turning-point from those years of desperation towards a new future and a new hope that was filled with the presence and promise of a God who cared enough even to give me sweet-smelling lavender! Treasure those extra-special times that God gives you; never forget them when the going is tough and you need to remember yet again how much God cares about the extra details in your life. What God did yesterday he will surely repeat in different ways again and again, giving fresh hope and joy when the circumstances seem so bleak. We have a God who delights to give the extra touch! I still look back on the sight of that lavender-filled drawer many years ago, when I need to remember in today's difficult circumstances that our

God knows and cares yesterday and today and for ever! Remembering helps me to be reassured and encouraged for today when circumstances are different but still difficult.

ELEVEN

'I Need You to be More Available'

I stood on the spot which I will always remember in the church hall having just come out of a church service. I was idly looking at a noticeboard while people walked past me when I suddenly heard the Lord speaking so clearly to me! I could not mistake his voice as he stood close beside me there: 'I need you to be more available.'

'But, Lord,' I faltered, 'teaching is so busy – probably sixty hours a week – and I invite international students to lunch most Sundays; how can I spare more time?' Nevertheless his voice was so clear that I knew I could not ignore it. I stood there, rooted to the spot, and yet I did not realise immediately that this was going to be a major turning-point in my life. It was the beginning of the autumn half-term break, so I went home and phoned my dear friends in Lancashire to ask if I could come and talk this new direction over with them. 'Yes, come!' they said, and so that week I headed north for quiet discussion with them.

It seemed to be just the wrong time family-wise; but it was amazingly the right time with the Lord! In the night the Lord gave very clear direction and I could share in the morning over the breakfast-table a clear calling to retire from teaching after the following summer. It would mean leaving teaching early with a smaller pension, but by the time I returned to Birmingham at the end of half-term I knew what I must do! And so on the Monday morning back at school I asked for the earliest possible appointment to see my headmistress.

My headmistress was genuinely shocked but realised my mind was made up. I offered to hand in my resignation in writing immediately so that the post could be advertised. So I did just that at the beginning of December for there was a certainty about this calling that I could not mistake.

Yes, there were times of encouragement, especially from individual friends, as I faced the enormity of what I had done. I was bringing to an end a career that I had genuinely enjoyed for many years and the future was so unknown, apart from a calling from the Lord I loved and trusted. But in all honesty there were also times of doubt and wondering where I was going next – if anywhere. Where would I start? What would I do? I had committed myself to an uncharted path. Had I really heard the Lord speaking when I could have been teaching – very happily – for another five years and building up my pension? Was I just imagining the Lord speaking to me? And would he speak so personally like that to me, just an ordinary, run-of-the-mill Christian who happened to be walking across the church hall one Sunday morning?

But the Lord kept giving small signs that this was from him. International students and their families were increasingly coming across my path. Encouraging letters were arriving from countries across the world. If only I had eyes to see, the rightness of the decision to retire was being confirmed again and again, but panic often made me blind. Sometimes there was a sense of excitement at the change of direction and the calling over my life. Yes, God was good in spite of my unfaithfulness and fear. There were people who encouraged for the future. Then there were events that showed time and again God's hand in this change of direction. I was told that my educational pension could be increased from years back, and it was obvious that the Lord would provide financially. Finance wasn't quite such a problem as the bigger issue of the whole new life-direction I was facing. I would be leaving a very fulfilling career that included rich social relationships on a daily basis, and I would be launching out on my own. Was this the right way ahead?

The Lord was so gracious in giving me touches of his reassurance. The extra pension I was offered from way back meant that the 'lump-sum' I was given would exactly pay off my outstanding mortgage and leave my home mortgage-free – an amazing gift from such a heavenly Father. Then my school asked me to teach two mornings a week in order to complete teaching some examination classes the next year, so the break was not quite as sharp as it might have been. I retained a small link with the world that I had known for so long just one more year.

But the plunge into a totally new life was still staring me in the face as I said my 'good-byes' to colleagues and pupils. It was either madness or a calling on my life that I could not neglect. I knew in my heart that it was the latter, but at times I struggled with the former interpretation. But there was no turning back now.

TWELVE

Getting Going

I finally 'retired' in the summer of 1994 and sought to leave my teaching career at the Lord's feet, where it belonged. There was encouragement from many, but trite, unnecessary remarks from others. I was tired, but I actually finally enjoyed retiring. I went up north to dear friends to unwind and find all the stress and strain of the end-of-term falling away to be followed by a tangible endowment of peace. I found rest, relaxation, unwinding and fellowship as the Lord began to turn my life around. At the same time I longed to see the whole family set free from so much that was oppressive. It would be so easy to say that the Lord answered every long-held prayer for family members at that time, but he didn't and I felt left to face my new future largely alone as far as the family was concerned. Changing direction may sound exciting, but it is also challenging as one wonders just how it will work out. It should have been a time of trust and peaceful anticipation for a future to which God had so clearly called me, but it wasn't quite like that! There were times when I wondered what I was doing, and the familiar life of teaching seemed infinitely preferable. This was one of those turning-points that was hard to accept. I was really on my own and not quite sure where to start. So often, it is when we are at the end of our own resources and plans that God steps in to show us the way forward. Some friends made comments that just gave a touch of the much-needed encouragement.

I began to meet up with overseas wives, and I knew from many years previously that these could often be the most lonely of all international folk around. Often with small children, with husbands working long, stressful hours, bereft of extended family back home, struggling with a different culture and a different language, they could be the most needy here. It seemed right to reach out to them in the weekdays, wherever they came from and whatever their faith or lack of faith. So that autumn we began an international wives' group here in my home.

There were two wives to start with, one from West Africa and one from Taiwan. They soon brought two others, and then that increased to eight. We quickly realised that a meal at lunch-time helped to settle people as they talked to one another round the dining-table. The freedom and joy was God-given and a delight to share. In the afternoon we started a very simple Bible study in English, followed by a cup of tea and biscuits before wives went to collect their school-children. We welcomed pre-school children here. It was a question of seeking God's way forward a step at a time.

There were plenty of diversions, notably from family members, not all of whom were supportive. And, as the background to new beginnings, my mother was ill in Cornwall, and this involved long journeys to visit her and settle her. But at the same time there were promises of financial support that suggested that what I was doing was touched by God himself. And there were increasing contacts with so many overseas students and a deep, underlying peace about the right way forward.

The number of wives coming for Bible study steadily increased and there seemed to be such freedom and joy amongst them. There seemed to be such release as we met in my home. We finished that first term with a Christmas lunch – and the promise of more help next term. It looked as though a pattern would be established for the future. As I looked back to those early days I saw so much of the goodness of God – a God who will lead us forward if we will just trust him, even when the going seems so impossibly difficult. And who was I to expect blessing in this way? But he who had begun a good work was going to complete it! I had no idea how or for how long; I could only trust him for the years ahead.

THIRTEEN

Using one's Home

One thing I knew for sure as I faced this new ministry was that it would be based in my home. This home had been used to raise four children who by now had basically left the nest – though not always entirely! From time to time some of them reappeared, with or without new families.

Now I realised how perfectly my home was placed for this new ministry. It was just a short, straightforward walk from one of the main gates of the University here, so very easy to find and in an area that was becoming increasingly lived in by students, both internationals and others. I was ideally placed to offer 'open home', and that was what I began increasingly to do.

Sunday lunches have always seen different nationalities round the dining-room table, but now I considered seriously the rest of the week, for which I had left teaching. I knew from far-off Ghana days that the loneliest internationals in Britain were those with small children whose husbands were busy studying for further degrees, while they themselves were bereft of extended family and friends back home. They found themselves in a largely unfamiliar culture and battling with a climate that was too often cold, wet and inhospitable. It could be incredibly lonely and demoralising. How could I help to meet a part of this need? I decided to try a Wives' Club in my home, but would they come and would it work? Tentatively I looked for likely contacts. I met one Taiwanese Christian wife who had just arrived and seemed interested. I went outside to post a letter and met a West African wife there in the road who said she would like to come. We arranged to meet and discuss the way forward.

FOURTEEN

It's Tuesday – Do Come And Join Us

The homemade soup is simmering gently in the kitchen and the dining-room tables are laid for sixteen. There is homemade bread, cheese and salad ready on the table. It's about12.45pm. and wives begin to appear, often with little ones in pushchairs. 'Come in and welcome!' Often it is warmer inside than outside. Coats and scarves are taken off in the hall. 'This is a friend of mine who would like to come and join us'. 'You are very welcome too. Just put a name-badge on so that everyone else knows who you are and which country you are from.'

By one o'clock people are finding a place at the table, having been asked which soup they and their child would like. Thanks for the meal is said by one of the leaders and then everyone is free to help themselves to what is on the table. Conversation gradually begins as people 'unwind' and soon it flows. No one must feel left out. Others will inevitably come late. Hopefully – and prayerfully – there will be enough soup to go round. We have never really run short yet. It is so good to see people begin to enjoy each other's company. There is so much to talk about! There are second helpings of soup for those who wish.

Then the tables are cleared, the dishwasher is filled and we are ready for the afternoon activity. Children go with a helper to the sitting-room where there are toys and even a viewing of 'CBeebies'.

Today a kind friend is going to demonstrate a particular kind of card-making, which is always popular. Soon pictures and backing-materials are chosen and a relative hush descends as everyone is involved in using her craft skills. Some beautiful cards are made to be used for various later occasions, or just to send to a friend across the world.

Before people need to leave to collect older children from school, there is a cup of tea and homemade biscuits. Some people have to leave a little earlier because they have further to go to collect school-children. Others stay to help to clear up the inevitable mess, but it is amazing how quickly willing hands and a powerful vacuum-cleaner restore the house to its previous state! People can be very helpful in working together. Three dishwasher loads usually complete the washing up. I am so grateful for modern technology.

'See you next time,' they call cheerfully as they go out of the door. And when everyone has finally left I can thank the Lord for another session that has brought people closer together and helped to relieve some of the loneliness and aloneness that many feel.

We learn a dance in the garden, making the most of a warm, sunny day.

Refreshment-time in the garden, when everyone can feel included and cultural barriers are being broken down.

Much enjoyment round the table when no one is excluded.

The move to my new flat meant that 'internationals' moved as well, and soon found that they were still at home even in new, more confined, surroundings. Life goes on!

Photographs by Lee Tze Theng (Joyce)

FIFTEEN

Setting a Pattern

Gradually a pattern began to emerge that has been with us for the past sixteen or more years. We needed several leaders to help to run events and also to look after a considerable number of pre-school children who needed not only to be safe here, but also be happy and want to come again! A crate or two of suitable toys was also needed. Then it became obvious very soon that a hot meal would settle people when they first came, so we developed a custom of cooking home-made soup and bread for lunch. It meant that everyone could settle down and enjoy a meal together before we did anything else. I think I was the only person I knew who extended my dining-room after my family had left home! But it was worth having a comfortable room where three dining-tables could be put end-to-end for at least sixteen to sit for lunch.

On Tuesdays it was good to plan out a varied social programme that attracted different wives. We planned this programme for school term-time, for crawling babies do not mix safely here with boisterous ten-year-olds! We have not got the space! We had just two rules – that only English was to be spoken, for that would help to improve everyone's English and would also prevent little cliques of different language groups. And we said 'No politics'.

On Fridays we again offered a hot lunch and then simple worship led by one of the wives and a Bible study led by one of the leaders, but open for any to share in, and it was always very relaxed. Then we have always made time for people to share their prayer-needs before we have a cup-of-tea and homemade biscuits. It works! Wives, both Christians and non-Christians, seem to be very open and enthusiastic and come back. There are those who have many years of Bible-knowledge and mainly want fellowship and those who say they have never opened a Bible before! All are equally welcome. There are those who have a vital, living faith and those who come because they want to know what the Christian faith is about. It is thrilling when someone says: 'What makes this place so different? I can feel a warmth as I come through the front door – and I don't mean the central-heating!' We have prayed beforehand that the warmth of the Lord's presence would be felt by all who come in. Prayer makes all the difference!

At the end of each term we hold an international lunch to which we invite all who have helped us, and when we ask each wife to bring a dish from her own country to share with others. What a variety of wonderful food from so many different countries, and what an opportunity for wives to thank those who have provided for them during the rest of the term – for we never ask otherwise for any contribution, for there are those who are well-off and those who are scraping just to keep going.

SIXTEEN

Seeing Individual Lives Blessed

Any group is made up of individuals, some of whom stand out as strong characters and some who are quieter and gentler until they begin to unwind and feel more secure within a group like this. Some are so easy to come alongside and others are harder to come to know. Some have been here relatively recently, while others have long since returned to their own countries and either keep in touch or have lost contact for some years. Amazingly, some have suddenly renewed contact by email or letter or telephone: 'I'm just calling from Terminal 4 waiting to board a plane home, but next time I'm here for a conference I'll make time to come and see you all in Birmingham.' What a joy that is! Someone from West Africa still remembers us after many years.

Many go back to their own countries. Would they go back feeling that their time in the United Kingdom had been largely wasted spiritually, or would they be rejoicing to know that what they had found here would be put to good use back home? One couple with children have settled in a church back in Korea where they have such a caring ministry amongst the poor and often neglected in their own country. 'We have learnt the skills and the calling for this while we were living on the edge of poverty studying in Birmingham', they say, 'and we are so much more fulfilled than if we had tried to go into a large, wealthy church.' That rejoices my heart. They have largely stayed in touch and I hear how their ministry as church leaders is so blessed.

Others we have inevitably lost touch with and occasionally that is heartbreaking. For example, the Chinese wife who became a committed Christian here and then her husband was struck with cancer. How we all prayed for this family with small children as well, and how she prayed for the miracle of healing, but her husband died and then we heard that she had denied in bitterness the faith that she had received over here. Where she was we didn't know then, but we longed to hear of a faith that was renewed and even deepened because of what she had had to face. We prayed on. One of our leaders here tried to find her when she visited China, but without success. It is never easy, but it is always possible to see faith blossom and flourish once more, even in the most desperate circumstances. We have an amazing God who never wastes the circumstances of our lives. We have since heard of a faith renewed and deepened and have recently met a radiant, restored woman when she came to visit over here and give a testimony of how God had met her again in an amazing way in her homeland of China.

There are some wives that just seem to be 'extra special'. Some years ago an Indian Christian couple went back to work in north India and then we heard that the younger of their two boys became very sick. They had to travel backwards and forwards to Vellore Hospital in south India for treatment. The journey alone was 2½ days. Much prayer was made here. Eventually Toby died and we wept with this family across the continents. Their faith weathered that desperate time, and now, much later, they have a new member of their family and we can rejoice with them. They are still in touch and have an open home with a very real testimony where they are in north India. They also welcome 'internationals' where they are on a university compound there.

One Taiwanese wife was too busy to make time for God. How we prayed that she, a so-called Christian, might find the time she desperately needed, and then she suddenly made contact with us again when she realised the need to make time for God each day, in spite of a very busy life. How we rejoice and pray that she will continue to find that space to hear the God she needs to come to know more carefully. She says that she will!

A wife from Mexico arrived in the group without a word of English. We had to 'borrow' a Spanish-speaking friend to help us at first to make contact. But the wife concerned was very determined to learn English and in a short space of time was picking up basic English and, being of a very outgoing nature, by the time she went back to Mexico, her English was fluent. What a joy she was, once she had gained confidence in English. She could mix so easily with others here, and she had a spirit that was very infectious, full of fun and laughter. Mexicans seem to have a special joy to add to the group and we are so grateful for several of them.

A Chinese wife has walked in recently and said as she came in for the first time, 'So how do I become a Christian then?' What a joy to explain and to encourage her to keep coming, which she is doing. Now she is asking about repentance!

We can celebrate with many members of the group. A much-longed for pregnancy is a joy to so many of us to share, and we wait eagerly for the due date later in the year. The passing of an English examination, the success of someone's child at school, a thrilling visit to Italy – 'they don't speak English there, you know!' – are all reasons for celebrating together and sharing with one another. A Latvian wife wrote the following:

'It is also a privilege of a very different kind to share in the hard times when things don't seem to be going right and others in the group can sympathise that they have faced similar difficulties. When it is cold and raining and you are stuck in a small flat with young children, then that is hard in a foreign land with no outlet. No one else seems to be outside when it is raining and it can be incredibly lonely and frustrating in those circumstances. There is a longing for adult companionship to while away the weary, rainy hours! Are anybody else's children just as difficult as one's own on a wet day?'

SEVENTEEN

Hindrances along the Way

In the midst of so much blessing and encouragement with international families I suddenly found myself struck down with one trouble after another that seemed to hinder so much of what God had surely called me to do. I had had cancer, but that had been caught early and seemed to have cleared. But then out of a 'clear blue sky' came epilepsy – maybe a side-effect of a drug I was on? – no one seemed to know. This was far more devastating even than previous illness because it stopped me driving, so I could no longer just pop in to see someone who needed visiting or do the odd bit of shopping or offer someone a lift, and it sometimes frightened me and made me far more dependent on others, especially family members. Then I had a fall – nothing to do with the epilepsy – that made me rather crippled for some weeks and dependent on all that the National Health Service could offer! And I, who had always been so independent found myself in a totally different situation, needing to be waited on and cared for. We had officially closed the Wives' Group that summer, but Wives kept coming. They were lonely and bored during the summer holidays and still looked for an 'open door', so sometimes, when they came, they even clashed with the visit of the district nurse, who must have wondered what was going on in my home! Why does God allow such sickness? I don't know. But I can only believe that he, who is so faithful, will make his purposes ultimately known.

I thought this group had finished the summer before last, but it seemed it was not to be so.

Yes, it is scaled down, but Friday afternoons are building up again with much encouragement. God spoke so clearly to me recently, and I accept this from him – 'Do not think that I have finished using the gifting I have given you.' So we press on! In the meantime I could only grieve and seek other people's help and support, which I don't always find easy as a very independent person. I can sympathise with others going through one trial after another, but I had always expected to be 'fit and well' in order to be ready for others, and now I was far from fit to reach out to those in need. And yet I was still finding myself drawn alongside those who needed a listening ear and just the right word for a difficult situation. Someone at my church had said: 'You know, you are like a magnet for internationals in need'. I was not that magnet in my own strength, but I acknowledged that God was still using me to reach out to those I met who needed encouragement and support. So many faces lit up as I stopped to listen and offer some prayerful advice.

In spite of all the difficulties of starting a 'Wives' group' again, it seemed that that was what God had in mind. Numbers were building up again and enthusiasm was growing. People that I didn't know were asking if they could join us, and we could not close the door – not yet, anyway! I thought we had reached that point, but God obviously still thinks otherwise! We were left with a skeleton staff of helpers, and I with a certain lack of energy, but God is right in the midst of us, blessing and encouraging and bringing new 'internationals' as well as the faithful few over many years. We wonder what the next step is, and God just says 'Follow me, and I will show you the way'. Do we sometimes have to learn the same lesson over and over again? I think that that is so. I thought I had learnt to trust God no matter what happened, and here I am having to learn to trust all over again. The situation is slightly different, but the learning-process is the same. I kneel at the feet of the one who comes so close especially when the going seems so tough, and he still whispers: 'You are precious and honoured and I love you.'

So I rejoice in all the encouragement that comes my way, and I pray for the energy, both physical and spiritual, that I still need for this calling. Yes, there are so many ongoing relationships that encourage for such a time as this. I have to learn to look for the encouragements rather than the set-backs that inevitably come my way. Just when I feel like giving up and relaxing into a cosy armchair called 'retirement' I am given an amazing touch of encouragement to keep going either by letter or email or phone-call. So here I am, still pressing on!

EIGHTEEN

Upheaval

By the winter before last it seemed right to try to sell my home of 36 years, scale down and move to a smaller, easier environment. The family was very keen for me to do this while I still had the strength and energy to be actively involved and make my own wise decisions. In the middle of the 'credit crunch' was not the best time to try to sell my dearly loved home, but eventually a buyer was found – even though at a very reduced price – and I was able to buy a pleasant 'retirement flat' nearby. Turning out and scaling down was much more difficult than I had thought, but it was amazing how someone always needed what I was discarding! Nothing was wasted, which was wonderful. I would have felt very sad to waste anything that I had treasured over the years.

I finally moved in the March, several months after the beginnings of negotiations. One of my sons stood in my empty house and said quite emotionally that it just wasn't 'home' any more. The other end looked like chaos for a while, but I was determined to make it my new 'home' as quickly as possible for everybody's sake. Things gradually fitted into place, a new colour scheme was chosen throughout and more than I expected was spent on improvements – for the first time for many, many years I had some spare cash! The place slowly began to look like 'home'.

The Lord had clearly told me just before the move that he had not finished using my gifting yet. So after the first week we began a scaled-down Bible study meeting for international wives again. They started to come back, at first pining for the home of previous days that they felt they were missing. Then after a few weeks one of the wives suddenly said: 'This feels like home now!' I rejoiced, for I longed still to have an open door for all who wanted to come – and they were here! We started a new Bible Study series and 'wives' came and went. Maybe we feel we have even more freedom than before. Certainly there is just as much laughter and joy and close, caring friendship. I am learning that the size of the house does not matter. If the genuine warmth of welcome is there, people will come. They are here again! A squash in the sitting-room, with some more agile wives sitting on the floor, works well. Maybe more relaxation than ever has led to everyone taking part and sharing in the Bible studies. Inevitably we still have sad farewells as wives return home or move to other parts of the country, but new wives appear as well, and seem determined to stay with us week by week. So we see lives changed and new friendships formed.

NINETEEN

God Who Blesses

Many times when life has seemed particularly rough I have stood in front of a picture that still hangs in my bedroom here. It shows a very dark, stormy scene, but right across the picture is a rainbow, and the words in one corner: 'God keeps his promises'. I have to remind myself of that again and again when events in life seem darker than ever. I know deep down that God is amazingly faithful and incredibly near when I need him. I can look back over many years and remember how time after time God has seen me through when the way ahead looked impossible for one reason or another. He has given me the spiritual gifts that I have needed for this ministry to which he called me. When I thought of giving up international wives' work as I was about to move into this flat nearly two years ago now, he spoke to me so clearly: 'I have not finished using your gifting yet'. So I still press on!

I am so blessed by my church fellowship that is lively and outreaching to others, and I find warmth and encouragement there. I also meet many 'internationals' there, so I can say: 'God is good' and I can rejoice in all the cross-cultural fellowship that I enjoy week by week.

But above all I know that the Lord himself is walking right beside me day by day, speaking to me and replenishing so faithfully all that he has called me to give out to others. Yes, this God uses all that we are sometimes called to face to bring encouragement and blessing to others who are finding life so hard. We can come alongside such people and point them to the one who is always there to lead us through to a new closeness to himself however dark the way. Whatever particular trial we may personally face, God never wastes what we have gone through, but can use it in amazing, unexpected ways, and bring positive blessing, not only to ourselves, but to many others whom we come alongside. I look forward to all that the next year offers, with a public recognition of this particular ministry that should bring even more encouragement to 'internationals'!

Praise the Lord, O my soul.
I will sing praise to my God as long as I live...
The Lord, who remains faithful for ever. (Psalm 146: 1–2, 6)
That is my testimony; may it be yours too! Jill Edgington.

Acknowledgments

I would thank both family and friends for all the help and encouragement they have given me, especially when inspiration has lagged over the years of writing.

Mrs. Barbara Ball carried out much proof-reading with skill and thoroughness as I sought to complete this manuscript. I owe her a great deal for her professionalism and patience.

I am very thankful to Canon John Hughes and Bishop Maurice Sinclair for their foreword and afterword to this book.

Those who have helped to lead the Wives' group at different times during the last 18 years have been such a blessing to everyone concerned. In recent years Gill Sinclair, and Carolyn Kemp and Mel Croom, both of OMF Diaspora Ministries, have given so much of their time and energy. This ministry is never a 'one-man band'!

I would especially thank Lee Tze Theng (Joyce) and Mui Teng Lau (Kym) for their photographic skills that have appeared in this book. There are also many others who offer photos that remind us all of past and present times and faces.

And, above all, I would thank the many international wives from many different nationalities, who have passed through my home. Without them, there would have been no ministry to write about. Their fun and laughter and deep searching for the truth have been such an inspiration to all who have been involved in this ministry over the years. I look at them, wherever they are, with great affection and amazement at what God has done in many lives.

Afterword by Bishop Maurice Sinclair

When the Lord said, "*Go and make disciples of all nations, teaching them to obey everything I have commanded you*", we might imagine that this exacting task was reserved for Christians who had never known self doubt or bitter disappointment. These super-men and women would be great strategists, making their plans for opening up some new frontier for missionary advance.

In a wonderful way Jill Edgington's story puts to rest this mistaken idea. If she is an unlikely missionary, aren't we all? Jill's experience of loneliness has equipped her in a special way for welcoming lonely people. The fact that time and again Jill had to depend upon the Lord to rescue desperate situations, has surely given her the edge in commending the Saviour to others. And what about those marvellous strategies for spreading the gospel? Jill makes no pretensions with regard to these; it is the Lord himself who includes her in a plan of his own making.

For her remarkable and sustained hospitality to visitors to Britain, Jill is a worthy recipient of the MBE. She is, however, a member of another 'empire': a kingdom whose King delights to use very human people in his purposes of love.

Bishop Maurice Sinclair
Honorary Assistant Bishop of Birmingham
February 2011